SUMMARY

&ANALYSIS

OF

BRAIN
FOOD

The SURPRISING SCIENCE of
EATING for COGNITIVE POWER

A GUIDE TO THE BOOK
BY LISA MOSCONI

NOTE: This book is a summary and analysis and is meant as a companion to, not a replacement for, the original book.

Please follow this link to purchase a copy of the original book: https://amzn.to/2GOygrF

TABLE OF CONTENTS

SYNOPSIS

In her book *Brain Food: The Surprising Science of Eating for Cognitive Power*, Lisa Mosconi reviews the connection between food and brain function and proposes changes people can make in their diet and lifestyle to achieve peak performance in everyday life and prevent, slow down, or halt the progression of Alzheimer's and other neurodegenerative conditions.

Drawing from her research and dozens of scientific studies, Dr. Lisa Mosconi challenges the pseudoscience disseminated by popular media and explains what foods like fats, carbs, and gluten do to the brain and gut.

The brain, Mosconi argues, has evolved differently from the rest of the human body, so it needs special foods to function optimally. She discusses how the brain is different in its composition and nutrient requirements and charts food plans that support a flexible and healthy brain. Vegetables, whole grains, legumes, plain water, and fish top the list of brain-healthy foods. Their conspicuous absence in the typical Western diet, Mosconi observes, explains the escalating incidence of neurodegenerative and lifestyle diseases like dementia and diabetes.

Mosconi notes that in addition to optimizing your diet, you can keep your brain active, slow its aging, and reduce your risk of mental conditions by taking on positive lifestyle changes that involve physical activity, intellectual stimulation, social interactions, and good sleep.

STEP 1: UNDERSTANDING NEURO-NUTRITION

CHAPTER 1: THE LOOMING BRAIN HEALTH CRISIS

Over the last two centuries, life expectancy across the globe has risen steadily. Today, most people in industrialized countries can expect to live to about eighty years. This achievement has been driven by improvements in standards of living. Vaccination, for example, has eradicated major diseases like polio, and improvements in housing and nutrition have lessened risk of contracting several diseases.

Longevity, unfortunately, has not corresponded with sustained health. Old age has become synonymous with debilitating diseases such as arthritis, respiratory problems, dementia and general age-related brain impairments. Even as more people in more countries continue to live longer, the burden of these ailments continues to grow.

Mosconi illustrates the escalating burden of age-related diseases with Alzheimer's because it is one of the neurological diseases approaching epidemic levels. There's a strong link between diet and the onset of Alzheimer's, so by comparing a healthy brain with one with Alzheimer's, it is possible to create a regimen that can help maintain optimal brain health.

Key Takeaway: The brain changes that lead to dementia occur over a span of decades.

Technologies such as DNA testing and brain imaging enable scientists to not only understand how the brain ages, but to identify people at risk of Alzheimer's years before initial symptoms appear. Current findings indicate that Alzheimer's occurs gradually over time and that the changes that lead to the disease begin as early as young adulthood. According to these findings, the brain changes that lead to Alzheimer's are triggered by genetic, lifestyle, and environmental factors.

"In other words, cognitive impairment is not a mere consequence of old age, but rather represents the endgame of years after years of accumulated insults to the brain" (Mosconi, Ch. 1).

Because it isn't a disease that occurs suddenly in old age, Alzheimer's leaves a lot of room for prevention. Positive lifestyle changes implemented early enough can prevent, slow down, or halt the progression of the disease.

Key Takeaway: It's often too late to treat degenerative brain conditions once symptoms appear.

Brain cells, unlike other cells in the body, are irreplaceable. Simply put, the brain cannot grow new neurons. Since neurons are susceptible to the natural wear and tear of aging, nearly everyone is at risk of degenerative brain diseases.

The brain is also naturally resilient. By the time damage becomes evident—by the time the symptoms of Alzheimer's begin to show, for example—the brain has taken so many attacks that it has exhausted its defense reserves. Because the damage is already done, current medication for Alzheimer's can only stabilize symptoms for limited stretches of time.

Alzheimer's is caused by an interplay of genetic, lifestyle and environmental factors, but most of the risk is non-genetic.

Key Takeaway: Your brain runs and dies on what you eat.

There's a significant connection between the foods people eat and their brain health. Over the last several decades, declining food quality—as animals are fed antibiotics, growth hormones and GMO feeds, and plants are raised in nutrient-deprived soils—has corresponded with the ballooning of cognitive degenerative conditions.

Of all your organs, the brain is the one most easily affected by a poor diet. The nutrients in food power cellular reactions and maintain brain tissue, so subsisting on a nutrient-deficient diet is a sure way to sabotage your mental health.

Proteins, for example, are broken into amino acids which prop up brain cells. Glucose, vitamins and minerals in whole grains, fruits and vegetables provide energy to the brain. Healthy fats, when broken into omega-3 and omega-6 fatty acids, ensure neurons remain flexible and responsive.

Mosconi includes MRI scans of two healthy people in their fifties to show the effects of diet on brain health. One of the scans belongs to a subject on a Mediterranean-style diet and the other to a subject on a western diet. The subject on the western diet, despite being two years younger, shows signs of brain shrinkage that would suggest she's older. Her brain has lost neurons, and the space left by shrinkage has been filled with fluids—a sign of oncoming dementia.

People on healthy traditional diets, it would seem, have fitter brains than those on unhealthy western diets, regardless of their genetic makeup.

CHAPTER 2: INTRODUCING THE HUMAN BRAIN, A PICKY EATER

The human brain, with its jelly-like consistency, is the most delicate organ in the body. Being the most vital organ, it is also the most protected. It is protected by the skull and by protective membranes called meninges. It is also immersed in cerebrospinal fluid, a liquid that cushions it from shock.

The skull, meninges, and cerebrospinal fluid only protect the brain from external harm. To protect the brain from internal threats, there is a blood-brain barrier: a network of blood vessels that prevents elements from entering the brain unless they are verified as safe and useful. The blood-brain barrier restricts toxins, bacteria and some hormones from making their way into the brain and, at the same time, gives a free pass to water, air and nutrients. By so doing, this barrier protects the brain from inflammation and infections.

Since prehistoric times, the human brain has more than tripled in size. Throughout upright man's seven-million-year history, major changes in the size of the human brain have corresponded with major changes in diet. Early man needed a diet dense in energy and fat to sustain the disproportionately large size of his brain. Since he didn't have the body size or skills to hunt game, he had to rely on fish, which are rich in the omega-3 fats that make up the brain, to meet his brain nutrition needs. Eating better increased the brain size of early humans, improved their skills, and made them smarter, bigger and faster.

Most of the energy-dense foods consumed by early man were plant-based. As early as 3.5 million years ago, grains like oat and wild wheat were a staple of early man's menu. Entire swaths of people subsisted on nuts, seeds, fruits, and vegetables. About 99 percent of the 5 million years humans have been on Earth, they have been hunter-gatherers.

The advances in farming and agriculture that took off about ten thousand years ago not only gave man steady access to food, they also led the way to radical changes in diet. Today's convenient foods and sedentary lifestyles have made man fatter, less muscled, and prone to lifestyle-related diseases like obesity and diabetes. Man's ancient body has not had time to adapt to the foreign and processed foods that make up the bulk of the modern diet.

CHAPTER 3: THE WATER OF LIFE

The nutritional needs of the brain are different from those of other body organs. Being a conservative organ, the only nutrients the brain allows to cross the blood–brain barrier are those nutrients it cannot make itself or cannot make enough of. Even so, it needs more than forty-five nutrients to function well.

The brain is also different from the rest of the body in composition. The body is 60 percent water, 20 percent protein, 15 percent fat, and 2 percent carbohydrates with only trace amounts of vitamins and minerals. The brain is 80 percent water, 11 percent fat, 8 percent proteins, and 3 percent vitamins and minerals with only traces of carbs.

Key Takeaway: Take 8 to 10 cups of water a day to keep your mind sharp.

Water is vital for the normal functioning of the brain because it is involved in each of the brain's chemical reactions. It carries oxygen, which supports energy production, and helps the brain absorb nutrients eliminate waste. In fact, water is so vital that a 3 percent drop in your brain's water supply can trigger symptoms of dehydration such as fatigue, headaches, brain fog and mood swings. Dehydration can even accelerate the brain shrinkage associated with dementia.

Drinking 8 to 10 cups of water a day can increase the brain's performance by up to 30 percent. According to research, keeping hydrated can increase your reaction time and speed up the pace with which you think, calculate, and complete tasks. One of the simplest ways to stay productive is to start your day with a glass of water. It counters the effects of an entire night spent without ingesting any fluids.

When you hydrate, try to drink spring water as it is usually high in minerals like magnesium and calcium. Beverages with caffeine, artificial sweeteners, or preservatives can promote rather than ease dehydration. Purified water cannot hydrate your brain because it has been stripped of the essential minerals that direct water where it is needed.

CHAPTER 4: THE SKINNY ON BRAIN FAT

About 11 percent of the brain's total weight is fat. Even without including the water content—and contrary to the popular notion that 60 percent of the brain is fat—less than half of the brain's dry weight is fat.

There are two types of fat in the body: storage (also called adipose or white fat) and structural fat. The body burns storage fat for energy and uses structural fat to build cells, fill the spaces between organs, and give the body structure.

All the fat in the brain is the structural type. Most of this fat is in the myelin, the fatty sheath that wraps brain cells to insulate electrical impulses as they travel around the brain. Fatty membranes also enclose neurons as a form of protection. The brain has no storage fat because presumably, the body would utilize this fat during starvation and sabotage the brain.

Although the brain contains fat, it doesn't need every kind of fatty acid to function well. The brain makes most of the saturated and monounsaturated fat it needs, so it doesn't need any more from external sources. It only needs to restock saturated fat when it grows new cells, and this only happens between infancy and adolescence. Some saturated fats in whole milk and coconut oil can enter the adult brain but only when they are needed.

The brain also makes its own cholesterol over the course of a person's formative years. Brain cholesterol is different from the blood cholesterol obtained from bacon, eggs, and other foods. Dietary cholesterol doesn't cross the blood–brain barrier, so by itself it doesn't affect brain function. It only affects the brain when it clogs arteries and limits the amount of oxygen that flows to the brain.

Key Takeaway: Take the right balance of omega-3s and omega-6s to stave off inflammation and cognitive decline.

The only fats the brain really needs are polyunsaturated fats such as the omega-3s and omega-6s found in eggs, fish, seeds, and nuts. These fats are essential because they make up most of the fatty acids in cell membranes in the brain. The brain does not make these fats in-house, so it has to obtain them from dietary sources.

A healthy immune system hinges on the balance of omega-3s and omega-6s. Omega-6 fatty acids are important because they have pro-inflammatory properties. Essentially, they help turn on inflammatory responses whenever there's an infection. Omega-3 fatty acids are anti-inflammatory—they help turn down the inflammatory response once the danger has been resolved. The ideal balance of these fatty acids in the body is two omega-6s to one omega-3. Too much omega-6s can trigger excess inflammation that can damage the brain over the long run and put the body at risk of inflammatory diseases like atherosclerosis and arthritis. The incidence of these diseases is escalating because most Americans take an excess of omega-6s in foods like bacon, chicken, and vegetable oils.

Omega-3s come in three types: ALA from plant sources like chia seeds, walnuts and sea vegetables; and DHA and EPA from fish like cod, salmon and mackerel. Black caviar has huge amounts of brain-building DHA and memory-boosting choline.

Omega-3s are especially important in fighting cognitive decline. Research indicates that more than 2 grams per day corresponds with a lower risk of developing Alzheimer's. MRI scans of elderly people on a diet low in omega-3s have shown signs of accelerated brain shrinkage. Consuming omega-3s on a regular basis has the added benefits of giving you more mental clarity and better ability to remember details and switch focus. The effects of omega-3s are strong if these fatty acids are derived from natural sources rather than supplements.

Mosconi recommends that people ought to consume at least 4 grams of omega-3s every day to keep their brains sharp and healthy. 3 ounces of wild salmon and a handful of almonds or walnuts is enough to meet this recommendation. A handful of peanuts or a few drops of grapeseed oil would be enough omega-6 for a day. To strike the right balance of omega-6s and omega-3s, swap beef and pork with cold-water fish: it has more protein, more omega-3s, and less omega-6s.

If you are a vegetarian, you can rest easy in the knowledge that phospholipids are mostly made up of omega-3s. Vegetables like cucumbers, sweet peas, and tapioca are rich in phospholipids, as are grains like whole wheat, barley and oats. The brain can get all the brain fat it needs from these foods. Current studies indicate that the monounsaturated fats in avocados and olive oil also support cognitive function.

Key Takeaway: Steer off saturated and trans fats to lower your risk of heart disease and dementia.

Saturated fat doesn't get a pass to the brain past adolescence, but excessive amounts of it can cause inflammation in the body and, consequently, reduce the amount of oxygen that flows to the brain. High intake of saturated fat increases the risk of type 2 diabetes and heart disease and, consequently, increases the risk of dementia. In one study of elderly people, researchers found that subjects who consumed the most saturated fat (more than 25 grams a day—about 6 slices of bacon) were up to four times more likely to develop cognitive decline than those who consumed the least amount of saturated fat (13 grams or less—less than three slices of bacon).

Trans fats have a near-identical effect on the body: they raise cholesterol levels, promote inflammation throughout the body, and increase the risk of heart disease and dementia. People who consume 2 or more grams of trans-saturated fats a day are twice as likely to develop cognitive impairments as those who consume less than 2 grams of trans fats. Processed foods like commercial donuts, biscuits, cookies, frozen pizza, and margarines are notoriously heavy in trans fats. Foods with hydrogenated fats in the ingredients—including French fries and fried chicken from fast-food joints, fried mozzarella and vegetable sticks—wreak havoc not just on your arteries, but on your brain as well.

CHAPTER 5: THE BENEFITS OF PROTEIN

Amino acids, the building blocks of proteins, are essential to the brain because they serve as neurotransmitters, help maintain healthy tissues, and power chemical reactions. The brain manufactures some amino acids on its own, so it doesn't need much of them from diet. Only essential amino acids—the ones the brain doesn't produce—are allowed to cross the blood-brain barrier.

The human brain has over 80 billion neurons—brain cells, so to speak—that send signals back and forth. Neurotransmitters carry electrical impulses from one neuron to the other and consequently, make thoughts, words and memories possible. Neurotransmitters play specialized roles depending on their chemical makeup, and abnormalities in a neurotransmitter affect the role it plays. Dopamine, one of the brain's neurotransmitters, affects attention, motivation and reward functions while serotonin influences mood, appetite and memory. When serotonin levels are low, people may develop symptoms of anxiety and depression. Dopamine abnormalities play a role in the development of schizophrenia, ADHD, and Parkinson's disease.

Key Takeaway: The foods you eat influence the creation of neurotransmitters which, in turn, run your mental operations.

The production of serotonin, for example, depends on how much of the essential amino acid tryptophan the brain gets. Common sources of tryptophan include chia seeds, spirulina, oats, milk, chicken, and fish.

To manufacture dopamine, the brain breaks down tyrosine, which is produced from the phenylalanine amino acid. High-protein animal products like beef, chicken and organ meats are rich sources of phenylalanine, as are plant-based foods like spinach, soybeans and nuts.

CHAPTER 6: CARBS, SUGARS, AND MORE SWEET THINGS

Neurons need a lot of energy to produce neurotransmitters and send signals to each other. Carbohydrates, mostly, supply the energy the body and brain need.

There are two types of carbohydrates: simple sugars like honey provide quick bursts of energy while complex carbs like whole wheat, which require more digestion, provide time-released energy.

The brain treats different carbs differently. "Sugar gates" in the blood-brain barrier open when the brain needs glucose and close once it has had enough.

Key Takeaway: Limit your sugar intake to the type and amount your brain needs to lower the risk of mental deterioration.

The brain relies exclusively on glucose for energy. Glucose is expended quickly, so it doesn't accumulate in brain tissues. Glucose deficiencies can halt brain function as happens when very low blood sugar causes the loss of consciousness.

White foods like bread, pasta, and baked goods are carbohydrates, but they have little of the type of sugar the brain needs. White table sugar, for example, is 100 percent sucrose—a kind of sugar the brain doesn't really need. Good carbs, like turnips, red beets, dates, grapes, and honey have plenty of glucose and little of other sugars. Turnips, for example, are 76 percent glucose.

The brain of the average adult needs about 62 grams of glucose in a 24-hour period. This is the equivalent of about three tablespoons of raw honey.

Mental sharpness rises and falls on the amount of glucose the brain gets. But too much sugar can wreak havoc on the brain. It can spike blood sugars levels and, over the long-term, cause insulin resistance. Eventually, perpetually high levels of blood sugar cause type 2 diabetes, which exacerbates the risk of dementia. Some studies have demonstrated that in elderly people, high amounts of sugar in the blood correlate with brain shrinkage, decreased memory performance, and the risk of dementia. Even blood sugars that the rest of the body can tolerate can be damaging to the brain. Unfortunately, typical American foods have too much of the sugars that contribute to mental decline and too little of the sugars that make people alert and smart.

Generally, good sources of brain-fueling glucose are foods that metabolize slowly and are high in fiber. Sugary drinks, candies, and white flour products metabolize quickly and are low in fiber. Complex carbs and starches like sweet potatoes, fiber-rich fruits like berries, and vegetables such as carrots take time to break down and do not cause the sugar spikes that sabotage bodily and mental health.

CHAPTER 7: MAKING SENSE OF VITAMINS AND MINERALS

Vitamins enable the brain to absorb and eliminate nutrients. They also supply the brain with the key it needs to unlock the energy in foods. Vitamins like B6 are essential in the production of neurotransmitters. Without these vitamins, neurological diseases may manifest or worsen. Deficiencies of vitamin B1, B6, and B12 can lead to dementia, and deficiencies in vitamin B9 can cause neural tube defects of the fetus.

Minerals such as iron, magnesium, and potassium give cells structure and help the brain regulate fluids and hydration. Iron facilitates the production of hemoglobin while zinc supports brain metabolism. However, overconsuming these minerals can harm the brain. Too much of zinc, iron, and copper can promote oxidative stress and contribute to cognitive problems in the elderly. Research indicates that too much of copper can cause accelerated brain aging, and these effects are worse in people whose diets are high in saturated and trans fats.

Key Takeaway: Most dementia cases can be prevented by increasing the consumption of B-vitamin foods.

The body cannot manufacture most of the vitamins it needs, so it has to take up vitamins from the food you eat. There are two types of vitamins: fat-soluble and water-soluble vitamins. Fat-soluble vitamins, which include vitamins A, D, E and K, can be stored in body fat and don't need to be continually replenished. Water soluble vitamins, including vitamin C, B12 and choline, cannot be stored in the body; they have to be absorbed from the diet every day.

Vitamins C and B12 support neurotransmitters and facilitate proper communication between neurons. The brain uses choline to make acetylcholine, a neurotransmitter which is crucial for learning, memory and reward. Foods rich in choline include egg yolks, fish, organ meats and peanuts.

Healthy B-vitamin levels can help guard against cognitive decline. In one study, elderly people whose diets were rich in folate (more than 400 mcg/day) were at a lower risk of developing dementia than peers whose diets were lower in folate. Similar findings have been reported for vitamin B12. In another study, supplementation with vitamins B12, B6 and folic acid was shown to reduce brain shrinkage and help maintain the memory function of elderly patients at risk of developing Alzheimer's. The three vitamins were most effective when taken with omega-3s fatty acids.

CHAPTER 8: FOOD IS INFORMATION

Human brains vary in shape, size, activity, and molecular composition. Most of these variations can be attributed to the unique genetic makeup of individuals, but lifestyle choices—especially diet—have a lot to do with the differences as well.

In this regard, dietary nutrients can be understood as signals that cells use to structure and maintain both brain and body.

Key Takeaway: Your genes turn on and off on your lifestyle.

Your lifestyle choices—including where you live, what you eat, and how you exercise—don't modify your DNA, but they modify the way your DNA works. The food you eat especially plays a crucial role in turning your genes on and off.

"The genetic lottery might determine the cards in your deck, but the way you are living your life deals you the hand you are actually playing. We're back to where we started— genes load the gun, but lifestyle pulls the trigger" (Mosconi, Ch. 8).

Key Takeaway: Healthy gut, healthy brain.

The brain is not as anatomically separated from the rest of the body as conventional wisdom would have you believe.

Recent research shows that changes in the gut microbiome can affect the risk of brain disorders such as anxiety, depression, autism and dementia. Microbes—the collection of bacteria, viruses, fungi, and other microorganisms that inhabit nearly every space in our bodies—influence everything from how you eat to what you think and feel.

Microbes help the body digest food and absorb minerals. Some bacteria produce essential vitamins necessary in the production of neurotransmitters. Some bacteria also make fatty acids that either strengthen or weaken the blood-brain barrier and, consequently, change what nutrients and foreign substances pass in and out of the brain. When pathogens cross the blood-brain barrier, the consequence could be diseases like meningitis.

Essentially, optimizing diet may help in the management of anxiety, depression, and other mental disorders.

CHAPTER 9: THE WORLD'S BEST BRAIN DIETS

Blue zones—the regions with the highest number of people who are a hundred years and older—include Nuoro and Ogliastra in Italy, Ikaria in Greece, Okinawa in Japan, and Nicoya Peninsula in Costa Rica. Although these regions have radically different cultures, they share similar lifestyles, and these lifestyles have a lot to do with their good health. For one, communities in the blue zones make physical activities such as walking, gardening or shepherding livestock part of their daily lives. They also prioritize relaxation, take regular naps, and maintain strong social connections.

The typical diet in a blue zone is largely plant-based. Carbohydrates make up the bulk of all meals, and the amount of proteins and fats served is usually low or moderate. Centenarians—the hundred-year-olds who live in these zones—stock up on legumes such as beans and only eat meat just a few times a month. Even then, meat is consumed in very small portions.

Two of the blue zones stick to a Mediterranean-style diet. Research indicates that people on this diet are less likely to develop lifestyle-related diseases like obesity, diabetes, and cardiovascular disease. They also have a lower risk of developing Alzheimer's and other cognitive impairments as they age.

Key Takeaway: People on a Mediterranean-style diet have healthier brains than those on a Western diet.

At the base of the Mediterranean pyramid are vegetables, beans, fruits, and nuts. These take up the largest portion of the plate. Above these foods are whole grains such as wheat, barley and oats, and above these is wild-caught fish. People on this diet take minimal meats and dairy. They use herbs and spices in place of fat and salt to flavor food. Their sweets, which are only occasional treat, are made from nuts and seeds and are sweetened with honey or molasses. Most foods are cooked in olive oil which has a high antioxidant content. Red wine, another staple of the diet, is also rich in antioxidants.

MRI scans of subjects on different diets indicate that people on a Mediterranean diet have healthier brains than those on diets high in red meats and artificial sugars and low in fish and plant-based foods. Brain scans of subjects on a typical Western diet show less activity and accelerated aging and indicate a higher risk of developing Alzheimer's than those of subjects on a Mediterranean diet.

CHAPTER 10: IT'S NOT ALL ABOUT FOOD

Your brain doesn't just function well on good food; it also stays healthier if it is regularly stimulated. Participating in sports, intellectual challenges, complex work, and socializing can help sustain cognitive function well into old age.

Key Takeaway: Exercise, get good sleep, and partake in social activities to keep your brain functioning at its peak.

The studies conducted on the effects of exercise on brain health haven't returned universal findings, but there's a strong case that elderly people who are physically fit perform better on reasoning and memory tasks than their sedentary counterparts. One study found that the risk of losing mental capacities among elderly people who took part in regular exercise like walking and bicycling was 43 percent lower than those who didn't.

Exercise, by enhancing blood flow and circulation, facilitates delivery of more oxygen and nutrients to the brain. Exercise also stimulates the release of endorphins, which make people more relaxed and in a better mood afterwards. Additionally, exercise stimulates memory formation and enhances immune system and enzymatic activity. This enhanced enzymatic activity has been shown to dissolve Alzheimer's plaques.

Exercise aside, studies have shown that regularly taking part in leisure-time activities such as gardening during midlife can reduce the risk of mental deterioration later in life. A sedentary lifestyle is a major risk factor in the onset of degenerative conditions because it ages the brain faster. As you age, your memory centers shrink and your mental sharpness reduces, and these effects are accelerated by a sedentary lifestyle.

You can also keep your brain sharper and healthier by engaging in intellectual exercises. Research indicates that people who retire early have an increased risk of developing dementia. Every additional year of work past retirement age has been shown to reduce the risk of dementia by 3 percent. Work not only keeps you active and socially connected, but it also challenges your planning, reasoning, and attention skills and improves your mental faculties. The activities you engage in don't even have to be all work; Intellectual activities like reading books, solving puzzles, and playing music can significantly reduce the risk of cognitive decline. In one study, playing board games reduced the risk of dementia among elderly subjects by 15 percent.

Aging well also has a lot to do with the social connections you keep. People with strong social support systems tend to live longer and better lives. Studies indicate that elderly people with strong social connections have as much as a 50 percent chance of living longer than counterparts with fewer social ties. It's worth noting that it is the quality, not the quantity, of these relationships that really matters.

Sleep is vital not just for staying focused, but for learning and memory consolidation as well. Sleep also helps clean the brain of waste products, free radicals, and toxins. The glymphatic system, which cleans the brain, fires up when you're about to get into deep sleep.

STEP 2: EATING FOR COGNITIVE POWER

CHAPTER 11: A HOLISTIC APPROACH TO BRAIN HEALTH

You can enhance your brainpower, improve your memory, and guard your cognitive skills by making simple dietary and lifestyle choices.

1. Increase your intake of brain-healthy nutrients and reduce your intake of harmful foods. Foods that affect the health of your heart such as fried, processed, and fatty foods, also harm your brain.

2. Change your lifestyle. Take on a healthy and engaging lifestyle with plenty of physical activity, intellectual challenges, social interactions, and sleep.

Key Takeaway: Lean toward a plant-based diet as much as you can.

Man, throughout most of his history, has subsisted on a plant-based diet. A plant-based diet isn't just the reserve of early man; it is the secret to longer and better lives today. The typical diet of communities with the highest number of centenarians is about 98 percent vegan with fresh, nutrient-rich vegetables, fruits, legumes and grains occupying most of their plates.

Plant-based foods are rich in all the vitamins, minerals, ant antioxidants your body and brain need. To ensure your brain is in its best shape, Mosconi recommends you make vegetables part of your lunch and dinner, take whole fruit at least once a day, and whole grains and legumes at least four times a week. To get healthy fats, top up these foods with high-quality fish at least two to three times a week. Pair fish with herbs to enhance its nutrients.

Limit your consumption of red meat, pork and cheese to no more than once a week. If you have to consume red meat, go for lean instead of fatty cuts.

For dessert, you can have dark chocolate as it is low in sugar and rich in minerals and antioxidant flavonoids. Look for chocolate with at least 65 percent cocoa instead of the typical milk or white chocolates that are full of sugar, fat, and additives.

CHAPTER 12: BE MINDFUL OF QUALITY OVER QUANTITY

The quintessential brain-healthy diet is composed of whole foods prepared from scratch, preferably by you.

The human body's ancient DNA—and its ancient brain— responds positively to whole grains, fresh, organic produce, and other natural plant-based foods. It also responds positively to wild-caught fish.

Key Takeaway: Focus on quality foods, preferably fresh, local produce from the farmers' market.

You can get quality foods without stretching your budget by shopping from online organic food retailers like Vitacost and Amazon. Whenever you can, avoid GMO products and choose organic especially when shopping for foods in the Dirty Dozen list. These foods, which include apples, tomatoes, potatoes and bell peppers, are, among all food categories, sprayed with the most pesticides. The Clean 15 foods, which include avocados, pineapples, cabbage and sweet potatoes, are safe and can be taken in their non-organic form.

Take 2 to 3 ounces of fish a day to get adequate brain-building DHA. Shop for wild-caught fish to avoid ingesting the pesticides, antibiotics and pollutants that go into farm-raised fish. Frozen wild-caught fish is still better than fresh, farm-raised fish. Wild Alaskan salmon, or mackerel, cod, and wild sardines are great additions to your meals.

Make fibrous and prebiotic foods part of your diet as they help ease digestive issues such as bloating, constipation and diarrhea. Prebiotic foods include garlic, onions, asparagus, and fermented organic milk. Fiber-rich carbs include cruciferous vegetables, oats, bran, and greens. Take a probiotic supplement if you only take prebiotic foods on occasion. Go for the probiotic with the most diversity, not the highest count, of bacteria it has.

Avoid pro-inflammatory foods as they accelerate the rate at which the brain ages. Highly acidic foods—especially highly processed foods with hidden sugars, trans fats, and empty sugars—are the most dangerous. Animal products like meat and high-fat dairy, especially when prepared in unhealthy oils, are also pro-inflammatory.

Key Takeaway: Watch how you eat as much as what you eat.

You power your body—and your brain—not only with what you eat, but how you eat. Vegetables, nuts, fruits and seeds are most potent when eaten raw because their phytonutrients work best when they are still intact. Sprouting whole grains and legumes—including rice, barley, and amaranth—help release more nutrients and makes them easier to absorb.

To get the most nutrients from fish and eggs, steam or poach and serve with fresh herbs. Roasting or grilling works well for meat. On the other hand, frying and broiling increases the inflammatory content of meat. Whichever method you use to cook, opt for unrefined oils such as the extra virgin varieties. Refining strips vegetable oils of their minerals and leaves them prone to oxidation.

Additionally, watch what you cook with; Chemicals in your cookware can leach into your foods and harm both body and brain. Metal poisoning from aluminum cookware and copper water pipes, for example, can lead to irreversible brain inflammation. Filter tap water with a high-quality faucet filter and get rid of aluminum, plastics, and synthetic nonstick cookware. Replace these utensils with stainless steel, cast iron, glass, or traditional ceramic cookware.

CHAPTER 13: A TYPICAL BRAIN-HEALTHY WEEK

Mosconi includes a "Brain Diet Pyramid" with guidelines for the types and quantities of foods to eat every day to achieve optimal brain health.

At the base of the pyramid is 8 glasses of plain water, a serving of low GI fruits like berries and apples, a serving of leafy greens, and a serving of whole grains, legumes and sweet potatoes. These foods and beverages make up the bulk of a healthy diet and should be taken at least once a day. Half a cup of plain yogurt or fermented vegetables should also be taken about once a day.

Higher up the pyramid, Mosconi includes fish or shellfish—a serving of which should be taken at least three times a week—and raw nuts and seeds, which should also be taken in the same frequency. Poultry or organic cheese should be taken at least twice a week and consumption of red meat should be limited to a maximum of once a week. A piece of dark chocolate between five and seven times a week can deliver a good measure of essential antioxidant flavonoids.

The other part of maintaining optimal brain health is limiting or eliminating unhealthy foods including all fast foods, white sugar and artificial sweeteners, red and processed meats, refined grains, processed dairy, sodas, and spirits.

Mosconi recommends that people should skip snacking rather than breakfast or other meals. Centenarians, after all, consider breakfast the most important meal of the day. A good breakfast should give your brain light, sustained energy, preferably from fibrous, glucose-rich foods such as whole grain, sugar-free cereal.

STEP 3: TOWARD THE OPTIMAL BRAIN DIET

CHAPTER 14: HOW BRAIN-NUTRITIOUS IS YOUR DIET, REALLY?

In this chapter, Mosconi includes a test anyone can use to gauge the overall health of their brain. The test, which mainly focuses on diet, also contains questions that touch on consistent or predominant behaviors like overeating, skipping meals, and snacking after meals. Questions range from, "How often do you eat read meat?" to "How frequently have you taken antibiotics since you were a child?" Test takers choose from among four answers ranging from "almost every day" to "rarely or never." Based on the score you get, you're either at a beginner, intermediate or advanced level.

CHAPTER 15: THE THREE LEVELS OF NEURO-NUTRITION CARE

In this chapter, Mosconi throws in specific recommendations tailored for people at each of the three levels of brain health.

People at the beginner level consume the largest amount of unhealthy foods. Often, their foods are loaded with refined sugars, trans fats, and empty calories. They hardly ever take brain-essential foods like fish, vegetables, whole grains and fruits.

People at the intermediate level are well on their way to optimal brain health. Those at the advanced level are as healthy as they can get.

Key Takeaway: At the beginner level, commit to gradually replace bad foods with good foods and then increase your intake and diversity of healthy foods.

If you are at the beginner level, the first thing you need to do is make fruits and vegetables part of your everyday meals. Take a serving (about a cup) of leafy greens like kale, spinach and collard greens or cruciferous vegetables like broccoli and cabbage for both lunch and dinner. Include onions, garlic and fresh herbs in your meals.

Throw out the frozen foods you are used to and opt instead for fresh organic foods. Canned and frozen foods don't have nearly the same amount of nutrients as fresh produce.

Take fresh berries and citrus fruits throughout the week to stock up on fiber, vitamins and antioxidants. You can start with a serving of these fruits a day. Snack on raw nuts and seeds and avoid the roasted, salted or processed varieties. Walnuts and almonds make for great snacks. Whenever you can, sprinkle flaxseeds or sunflower seeds into your soups and salads.

Have a portion of sweet potatoes two to three times a week. Sweet potatoes are rich in fiber, antioxidants, and vitamins B6 and C, and they help reduce your cravings for sweets. Eat a serving of whole grains like brown rice or oats twice a day. When you get a sweets craving, reach for a piece of dark chocolate and a handful of almonds.

Introduce fish to your diet to replenish the healthy omega-3s that keep your brain fit and stall the onset of diseases like Alzheimer's. Start with two servings of fish a week, preferably wild-caught varieties.

Cut back on your consumption of dairy, red meat, sweets, and fried foods, especially commercial cakes, donuts, and cookies which are almost always loaded with trans fats and refined sugars. Eliminate frozen dinners and other ready-made foods for the same reason. Products from commercially raised animals are harmful because the pesticides, toxins, and pollutants used to treat them end up in your body. These toxins increase inflammation in your body and wreak havoc on your microbiome.

Good choices for cheese are Parmesan, cottage cheese, and aged cheddar. Even if these are the good varieties, they should only be taken sparingly as a treat. The only dairy you should take every day is kefir or plain, unsweetened yogurt. A cup of yogurt a day fills your gut with probiotics and helps maintain optimal gastrointestinal functions, which circles back to a healthy brain. Replace pro-inflammatory vegetable oils like corn and sunflower oils with healthy unrefined or cold-pressed oils from olives, coconuts and avocados.

Keep hydrated to increase your reaction time and keep your brain running optimally. Replace milk beverages with healthy smoothies. You can make quick smoothies with coconut water, chia seeds, raw cacao, and berries. Flavor your foods with herbs and spices to eliminate the need for dehydrating table salt.

At the beginner level, you are most probably leading a sedentary lifestyle. It would be a good idea to include some form of physical activity in your daily routine. If you don't get much exercise, start by speed-walking at least twenty minutes a day and increase your pace and time as this exercise becomes a regular habit.

Key Takeaway: At the intermediate level, focus on quality and experiment more.

At this level, your diet qualifies as healthy, but it is not optimized for the health of your brain.

When you're shopping for your kitchen, don't just go for any vegetables or proteins. Choose organic vegetables and switch your protein sources from meat and dairy to fish, chicken, and plant-based sources.

At this level, the goal is to make fresh organic greens like dandelion greens part of your everyday diet. When you make a serving of vibrant vegetables like Brussels sprouts, fennel, zucchini and cauliflower part of your everyday lunch and dinner, you can boost your cognitive abilities to match those of someone eleven years your junior.

Since you are comfortable eating healthy, nonconventional foods, you can add more special foods to your diet for their anti-aging properties and other health benefits. Brazil nuts are a rich source of selenium, and caviar, chia seeds, and other superfoods are great brain-builders.

In addition to your regular fruit combo, take a serving of lesser-known berry varieties like gooseberries and goji berries every day. These varieties are rich in antioxidants and fiber.

At the intermediate level, you already eat nuts and seeds often enough. The goal here is to make snacking on the likes of walnuts, Brazil nuts, and pistachios a consistent habit. If you like your nuts roasted or toasted, do it yourself, and do it with healthy fats and minimal salt.

For your grains, try ancient varieties like amaranth, kamut, and buckwheat alongside your regular grains. You can also try products made with these grains. Served with lentils, beans and chicken peas, these grains pack about as much protein as your meats. These complex carbs are also rich sources of fiber, minerals, and vitamins.

Pay special attention to the quality of meats and dairy in your diet. As much as you can, ensure the fish you take three times a week is wild-caught. Supplement it only with lean proteins from free-range turkey, chicken, or quail. Even as you limit your consumption of dairy, opt for cheeses from sheep and goat milk as they're richer in calcium and PUFAs than varieties made from cow's milk. The amount of cheese you take in a week should not exceed 2 ounces.

When it comes to sugar, salt and processed foods, the goal here is to completely eliminate these foods from the diet.

Avoid foods that may not appear processed but in fact are. These include instant oatmeal, commercial fruit juices, and low-fat dairy. Use as much of balsamic vinegar or tamari as you like—it'll help you cut back on salt, which can increase the risk of high blood pressure and heart disease.

Try to vary the size of your meals. Have a good breakfast, a good-sized lunch, and make dinner your smallest meal. For even better health, start practicing intermittent fasting a few times a week. Have an early dinner (at about six) and avoid eating again until seven or eight in the morning. You can take as much water and herbal tea as you like during this period.

To stimulate your mind, incorporate brain-healthy exercises like cycling and swimming into your routine. Aim for a minimum of three forty-five-minute sessions of moderate intensity exercises a week. It'll improve your cardiovascular strength and brain fitness and slow down aging.

Key Takeaway: At the advanced level, optimize your lifestyle for maximum brain fitness.

At the advanced level, your brain would be considered "brain-nutritious." You love fish and eat it often (alongside fish oil or omega-3 supplements), you eat leafy greens every day, and berries and citrus fruits are a staple in your meal plans. You rarely or never eat white-flour breads, pastas or pizza, foods with trans fats, or soda and juices.

The focus here is to take on and maintain a lifestyle that resembles that of centenarian communities.

To begin with, introduce more organic wild greens such as watercress and Swiss chard into your diet and explore the likes of mustard greens, mizuna, and radicchio. Some of these wild varieties have been shown to have ten times as much antioxidants as red wine.

For your berries, look for seasonal varieties harvested from the wild. When fresh berries are out of season, stock up on citrus fruits such as grapefruits and oranges, and glucose-rich plums like Italian or Empress plums. Make sure you have a serving of fruit at least once a day.

Make the bright purple Okinawan sweet potato a staple of your diet. It is high in healthy glucose content, vitamin A and C, fiber, and manganese.

Invest in a small jar of black caviar so you can sprinkle some on your snacks or yogurt. Caviar is the "ultimate brain food" as it is rich in brain-healthy fats and has high levels of antioxidant vitamins, minerals, B vitamins, and essential amino acids.

In addition to your healthy oils—including cold-pressed flaxseed and avocado oils, with which you're already familiar—consider hemp oil. Its ratio of omega-6 to omega-3 is a perfect 3:1.

Since you are already comfortable with overnight fasting, take a step further and try the 5:2 fast. Eat normally for five days in a week and then, for the remaining two days, restrict your caloric intake to no more than 600. Fasting will reduce inflammation and insulin resistance and lower your blood pressure, cholesterol and triglycerides within just a few months.

For your physical stimulation, create time for one to two hours of vigorous exercise a few times a week. Whenever you can, try and make hiking part of your regular exercise. In addition to the physical exertion it gives you, hiking—through your interaction with nature—can ease stress and anxiety and improve your mental health.

CHAPTER 16: BRAIN-BOOSTING RECIPES

Whichever level of brain health you are at, some healthy recipes can fast-track your progress to optimal brain health. In this chapter, Mosconi includes dozens of simple recipes anyone can use to prepare brain-healthy foods at home.

For breakfast, try an avocado toast. You make it with a ripe avocado mashed and spread over toasted Ezekiel bread and then garnished with extra virgin olive oil and chili flakes. You can also try blackberry banana muffins: grind organic rolled oats and almonds to a flourlike texture, mix the dough with walnuts, chia seeds and baking powder, and add an egg and mashed bananas and blackberries to the mixture. Fill this mixture into cups and bake.

For lunch, try the Buddha Bowl. The Buddha bowl is a mix of kale, broccoli, beets and carrots steamed and combined with toasted almonds, tofu, and cooked wild rice and quinoa.

Nonna's dandelion greens are a great option for dinner. Place a pound of organic dandelion greens in a saucepan, cover with water, and cook over medium heat until greens are tender. Drain, scoop into a serving bowl, drizzle with olive oil and lemon juice, and add some salt to taste.

Alternatively, you can try the nutrient-rich essential vegetable soup. Take broccoli, red cabbage, carrots, scallions, celery, garlic cloves, all finely chopped, and throw into a large pot with some edamame, grated ginger, sweet peas and vegetable broth. Boil for 20 minutes, serve in bowls, and sprinkle a teaspoon of brewer's yeast in each bowl. Brown rice can give the soup more texture.

For a quick, healthy snack, try peanut butter power bites. Blend a cup of oats and half a teaspoon of ground cinnamon to a flourlike consistency. Add grapes, maple syrup, and peanut butter and blend until the mixture is doughy. Shape the dough into balls and roll into chopped peanuts. Refrigerate for an hour and serve.

EDITORIAL REVIEW

Lisa Mosconi's *Brain Food: The Surprising Science of Eating for Cognitive Power* comes at a time when entire generations are watching their waistlines and not nearly enough people are watching what goes into their most important organ. In this in-depth exploration of the biology and chemistry of the brain, Mosconi summarizes the latest research that links food and lifestyle choices to cognitive performance and decline and explains why eating right isn't all about getting a beach body.

Mosconi explains that the human brain is a delicate, energy-hungry organ with irreplaceable cells, so it needs extra care and nourishment to function well. It needs glucose from healthy sources like complex carbs, it needs fatty acids from quality fish, and it needs a good measure of vitamins and minerals from fresh, organic produce. In the absence of these nutrients, it shrinks, ages faster than it should, and manifests the irreversible symptoms of Alzheimer's and other neurodegenerative diseases.

Mosconi's central argument is that our brains—and our bodies—would be better off if we ate closer to nature, like our ancestors did, and opted for more fresh plant produce and fewer animal products. Some of the world's healthiest communities, she contends, are essentially vegetarian, save for the fish they eat a few times a week. These communities may have radically different cultures, but their foods are a lot alike. They regularly consume wild fresh greens and fresh fruits, both of which pack the vitamins, minerals and antioxidants needed to keep brain cells healthy. Other staple foods of these centenarian communities include nuts and seeds, local whole grains and beans, starches like sweet potatoes, and fish, especially fatty fish like salmon. They limit their consumption of red meat, dairy, and desserts.

Brain Food is different from other nutrition books in that it is not yet another worn-out recap of brain health and nutrition facts by an outsider. Mosconi has had training in neuroscience, integrative nutrition, and holistic health. She has spent 15 years doing research on the brain's interaction with food. Part of her research has involved the analysis of brain scans of people on different diets. But even with all her experience, she doesn't merely rely on her knowledge to stake her claims. Her book is well researched, and the evidence is at the back where there are about a dozen pages of cited works.

Written in simple prose for the general audience, *Brain Food* is easily digestible, comprehensive, and workable. Mosconi throws in some anecdotes to help explain the more science-y stuff and make her work accessible. She includes an in-depth quiz to help readers determine how healthy their brains are, makes specific food recommendations for people anywhere on the brain-health spectrum, and follows these recommendations with 24 delicious recipes. Mosconi's recommendations are workable because she acknowledges how difficult it is to change bad habits and goes on to suggest positive changes that can be implemented incrementally.

But for all her straight talk, Mosconi gives her book what—in the end—emerges as an overpromising title. A little of the science she covers is new and surprising, but there's nothing surprising about most of the recommendations she makes. That people should eat mostly plant-based foods, drink eight glasses of water a day, eat some fish, and cut back on refined sugar, processed foods and red meat isn't exactly news. Most of the book feels like a mere validation of what most people know about healthy eating, and there's a lot of repetition to boot. But then again, some reminders of healthy eating wouldn't hurt anyone.

All the same, *Brain Food* offers a new perspective on the relationship between what people eat and how their brains grow, function, and age. In the end, the core message is simple yet powerful: food is information, and food is medicine.

BACKGROUND ON AUTHOR

Lisa Mosconi is an Italian-American author, neuroscientist, integrative nutritionist, and associate director of the Alzheimer's Prevention Clinic at Weill Cornell Medical College. She is a former assistant professor at the New York University Department of Psychiatry.

Mosconi, who was born and raised in Italy, has a degree in Experimental Psychology and a PhD in Neuroscience and Nuclear Medicine from the University of Florence. She also has certification as a holistic healthcare practitioner and a holistic health coach in the US.

Mosconi has spent more than a decade using brain imaging techniques to detect the likelihood of developing Alzheimer's and to identify at-risk individuals. She has published more than 100 peer-reviewed papers in renowned medical journals and presented at over 80 international conferences. Her work has been featured on CNN, Forbes, the *Wall Street Journal*, and other major news and research outlets.

Brain Food: The Surprising Science of Eating for Cognitive Power is her first book.

END OF BOOK SUMMARY

If you enjoyed this *ZIP Reads* publication, we encourage you to purchase a copy of the original book from.

We'd also love an honest review on Amazon.com!

Made in the USA
Columbia, SC
12 February 2019